Ice Cream Cone Quilt

Eleanor Burns

To El,

Like Ice Cream, you add joy and smiles to so many people.

The quilting world is a happier place because of your sense of humor,

honesty and the positive attitude you share with everyone around you.

Thank you for giving me the opportunity to grow as a quilter

and for your continued support.

Love, Sue

First printing July, 2000

Published by Quilt in a Day®, Inc.
1955 Diamond St, San Marcos, CA 92069

©2000 by Eleanor A. Burns Family Trust

ISBN 1-891776-03-7

Art Director Merritt Voigtlander

Table of Contents

Ice Cream Cone Quilt with Chain Setting

Ice Cream Cone Quilt with Lattice and Cornerstones Setting

Triple Decker Pillow or Wallhanging

Happy Birthday Quilt

*Juanita Benoit
2019
Gueydan La
70542*

Introduction & Supplies

There are no artificial preservatives in these charming Ice Cream Cone Quilts - just pure natural ingredients of 100% cotton.
You can scoop up your favorite flavors of ice cream in Chocolate, French Vanilla, or Strawberry.

Or be daring, and scoop up flavors of Blueberry, Mandrin Orange, Butterscotch, Pistachio, or Peppermint.

The graceful melted look in the ice cream scoops is achieved with an easy applique method using light to medium weight, non-woven fusible interfacing, eliminating the need for freezer paper or needle turn.

What's your preference in ice cream cones? Do you prefer a traditional cake cone, or an old-fashioned sugar cone? Waffle cones are befitting for multiple scoops! Or select a colorful cone for a real party!

The Ice Cream Cone and Party Hat shapes are sewn with the Triangle in a Square technique. Triangle in a Square rulers are available so accurate cutting, piecing, and squaring can be accomplished easily.

There are three fun, light hearted lap robes to make, plus two smaller delightful projects. So now you have the scoop on Ice Cream Cone quilts. It's time to dig in!

 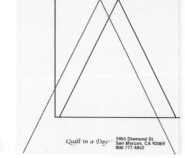

Triangle in a Square Rulers

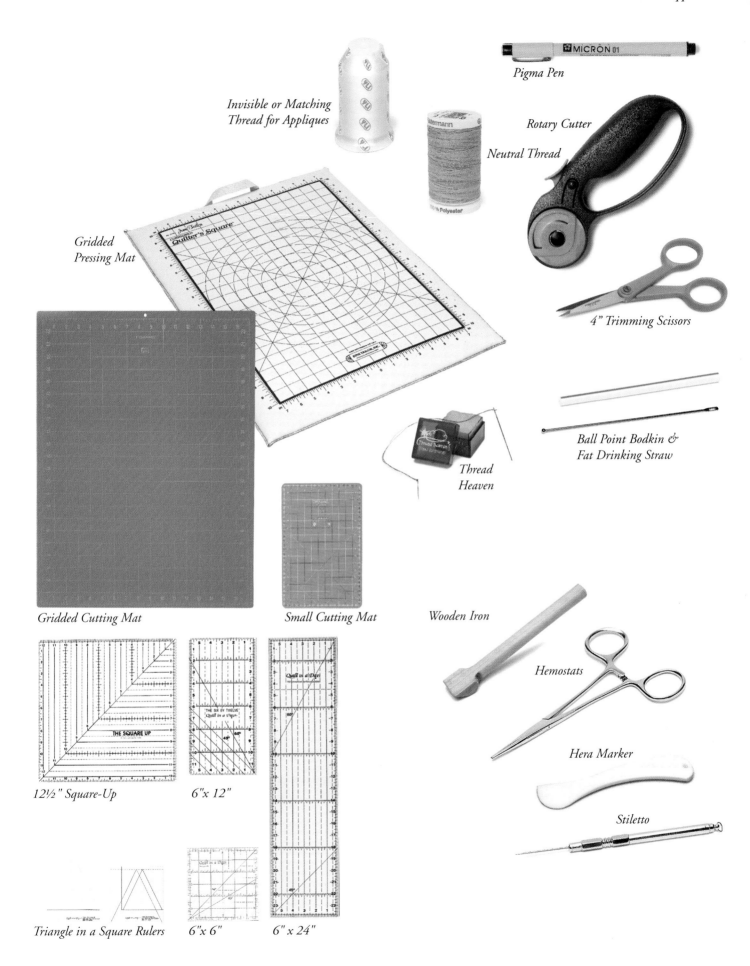

Pigma Pen

*Invisible or Matching
Thread for Appliques*

Rotary Cutter

Neutral Thread

*Gridded
Pressing Mat*

4" Trimming Scissors

*Ball Point Bodkin &
Fat Drinking Straw*

*Thread
Heaven*

Gridded Cutting Mat

Small Cutting Mat

Wooden Iron

Hemostats

Hera Marker

12½" Square-Up

6"x 12"

Stiletto

Triangle in a Square Rulers

6"x 6"

6" x 24"

General Instructions

Cutting Strips Selvage to Selvage

1. Cut a nick in one selvage, the tightly woven edge on both sides of the fabric. Tear across the grain from selvage to selvage.

2. Press the fabric, particularly the torn edge.

3. Fold the fabric in half, matching the frayed edges. Don't worry about the selvages not lining up correctly as this is not always possible. Line up the straight of the grain.

4. Place the fabric on the gridded mat with the folded edge along a horizontal line, and the torn edge on a vertical line.

5. Place the quarter inch line of the ruler along the torn edge of the fabric.

6. Spread your fingers and place four on top of the ruler with the little finger on the edge to keep the ruler firmly in place.

7. Take the rotary cutter in your free hand and open the blade. Starting below the fabric, begin cutting away from you, applying pressure on the ruler and the cutter. Keep the blade next to the ruler's edge. Cut off the torn edge.

8. Cut strips according to the yardage chart. Open the first strip and look at the fold to see if it is straight. If it has a crook that looks like an elbow, the fabric may not be folded on the straight of the grain. If this happens repeat the preceding steps.

Triangle in a Square Templates

If you do not have the Triangle in a Square rulers, make your own templates.

Triangle Shape

Cut a 5" x 5½" piece of template plastic. Trace lines with colored sharp markers and cut triangle shape. When indicated to use the triangle ruler, trace around the triangle template with a marking pen, and rotary cut on the lines with a 6" x 12" ruler.

Square Shape

Cut a 4½" square of template plastic, and trace lines. Tape the square template to the underneath side of a plexiglas 6" x 6" ruler and use as instructed.

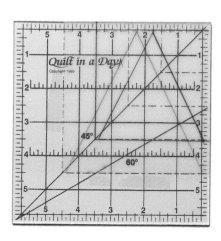

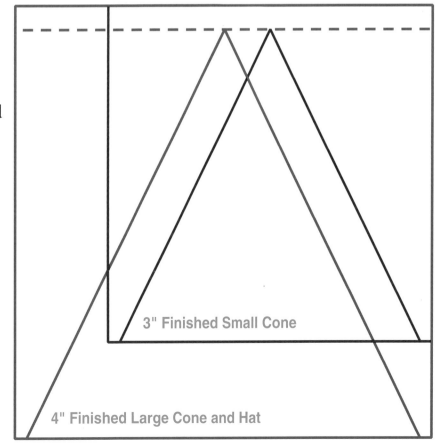

3" Finished Small Cone

4" Finished Large Cone and Hat

3" Finished Small Cone

4" Finished Large Cone and Hat

¼" Seam Allowance Test

Use a consistent ¼" seam allowance throughout the construction of the quilt. If necessary, adjust the needle position, change the presser foot, or feed the fabric under the presser foot to achieve the ¼". **Complete the ¼" seam allowance test before starting.**

1. Cut (3) 1½" x 6" pieces of fabric, and sew the three strips together lengthwise with what you think is a ¼" seam.

2. Press the seams in one direction. Make sure no folds occur at the seams when pressing.

3. Place the sewn sample under a ruler and measure the width. It should measure exactly 3½". If sample measures smaller than 3½", seam is too large. If sample measures larger than 3½", seam is too small. Adjust the seam allowance and repeat if necessary.

¼" Foot and Stitches Per Inch

Available for most sewing machines, the ¼" foot has a guide on it to help you keep your fabric from straying, giving you perfect ¼" seams. Your patchwork is then consistently accurate. Sew patches with 15 stitches per inch, or a #2 on computerized sewing machines.

Applique Foot and Stitches Per Inch

Use an open toe metal foot or foot with plastic bottom for applique and sewing on interfacing. Sew around Scoops on fusible interfacing with 20 stitches per inch, or 1.5 on computerized sewing machines.

Pressing

Throughout the quilt construction, it is important to set the seams, or lock the stitches, and then press the seams in a given direction.

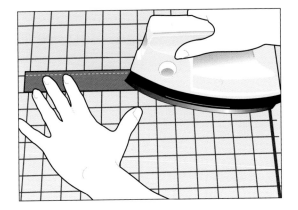

1. Before opening, lay the sewn strips or pieces on the gridded pressing mat. Line up strips with the grid to avoid "bowing." Place the strip on top that you want the seam directed to.

2. Press the strips to set the seam. The use of steam is your preference.

3. Lift the upper strip and press toward the fold. The seam will naturally fall behind the upper strip. Check that there are no folds at the seam line.

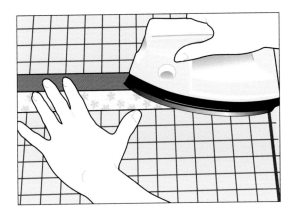

4. Turn the strips over. Check that the seams are pressed in the right direction.

Locking Seams

A general rule is to press the seams to the darkest side. However, some pieces have locking seams, so they may not follow that rule.

Pressing Flat Pieces

Pieces as the Triangle in a Square are pressed in the direction of least resistance so they lay flat. Follow the instructions for which way to press.

Pressing Applique Pieces

Arrange pieces and use a hot iron with steam to press in place until they adhere. Use an up and down motion with the iron so pieces do not move. Once pieces adhere on the right side, turn the piece over and press on the wrong side.

Use an electronic press or iron to fuse applique pieces.

Two Cone Quilts

Cones with Chain Setting

Cone Block

Make 14 Cone blocks
13 for the quilt top and
one for the label

Chain Block

Make 12 Chain blocks

Sue Bouchard   46" x 56"

Background Fabric			**2¼ yds**
Cone Block			
(1) 6" strip			
(3) 4½" strips cut into			
(14) 4½" x 8½"			
(6) 2½" strips cut into			
(14) 2½" x 8½"			
(28) 2½" x 4½"			

Chain Block
(2) 5½" strips
(4) 2" strips
(2) 2½" strips
(4) 3½" strips

7 different **Ice Cream Fabrics**   ¼ yd ea.
Cut from each fabric
Rainbow Border - cut first
(1) 2½" strip
Ice Cream Scoops
(1) 5" x 12"

Medium Fabric   1½ yds
Cone
(2) 5" strips
Chain
(8) 2" strips
(2) 2½" strips
First Border
(5) 2" strips

Batting (100% Cotton)   18" x 20"
Stuffing for Scoops

Binding   ⅝ yd
(6) 3" strips

Backing   3 yds

Batting   56" x 66"

Non-Woven
Fusible Interfacing   ⅔ yd

Cones with Lattice and Cornerstones Setting

Cone Block

Make 10 Cone blocks
9 for the quilt top and
1 for the label

Lattice

Make 24 Lattice

Cornerstone

Make 16 Cornerstones

Sue Bouchard   36" x 42"
or with Optional Border   44" x 50"

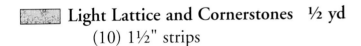
Background Fabric   1 yd
Cone Block
  (1) 6" strip
  (4) 2½" strips cut into
     (20) 2½" x 4½"
     (10) 2½" x 8½"
  (2) 4½" strips cut into
     (9) 4½" x 8½"

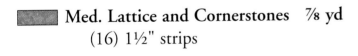
Light Lattice and Cornerstones   ½ yd
  (10) 1½" strips

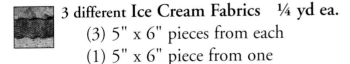
Med. Lattice and Cornerstones   ⅞ yd
  (16) 1½" strips

3 different **Ice Cream Fabrics**   ¼ yd ea.
  (3) 5" x 6" pieces from each
  (1) 5" x 6" piece from one

Cones   ¼ yd
  (1) 5" strip

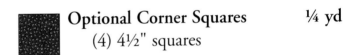
Optional Border   ¾ yd
  (5) 4½" strips

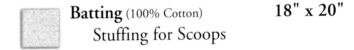
Optional Corner Squares   ¼ yd
  (4) 4½" squares

Batting (100% Cotton)   18" x 20"
Stuffing for Scoops

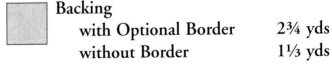
Binding   ½ yd
  (5) 3" strips

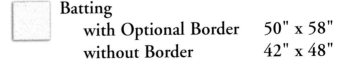
Backing
  with Optional Border   2¾ yds
  without Border   1⅓ yds

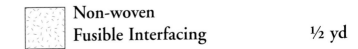
Batting
  with Optional Border   50" x 58"
  without Border   42" x 48"

Non-woven
Fusible Interfacing   ½ yd

Making the Cone

Follow these instructions for both the Chain and Lattice and Cornerstone settings.

1. Fold the 6" Background strip in half wrong sides together. **This step is essential for mirror images pieces.**

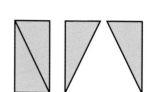

Fold

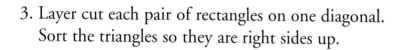

Cut 3" x 6" rectangles

2. With 6"x 12" ruler, layer cut pairs of 3" x 6" rectangles.

   Chain Setting - cut 7 pairs for 14 rectangles

   Lattice and Cornerstone Setting - cut 5 pairs for 10 rectangles

3. Layer cut each pair of rectangles on one diagonal. Sort the triangles so they are right sides up.

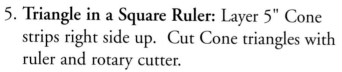

4. **Template:** Layer 5" Cone strips right side up. Trace Cone triangles on strip, turning each time. Cut with rotary cutter and ruler.

   Chain Setting - Cut 14 triangles

   Lattice and Cornerstone Setting - Cut 10 triangles

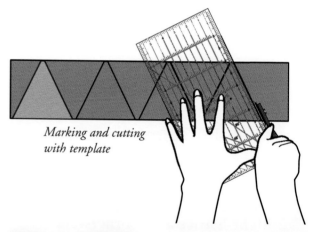

Marking and cutting with template

5. **Triangle in a Square Ruler:** Layer 5" Cone strips right side up. Cut Cone triangles with ruler and rotary cutter.

   Chain Setting - Cut 14 triangles

   Lattice and Cornerstone Setting - Cut 10 triangles

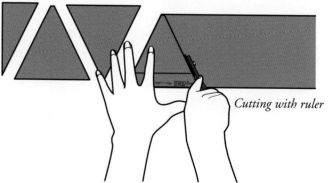

Cutting with ruler

6. Lay out Cone with the base at the bottom. Position Background triangles on each side of Cone. Make sure all fabrics are turned right side up.

7. Set the right Background triangle aside. Flip Cone triangle right sides together to left Background triangle.

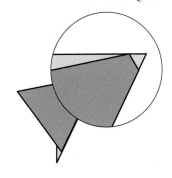

8. Position the triangles so Background fabric extends beyond Cone fabric at the top, creating a tip at the flat top.

9. Assembly-line sew with an accurate ¼" seam. Use stiletto to guide pieces.

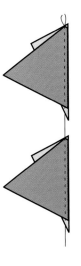

10. Set seams with Background on top, open, and press toward Background fabric.

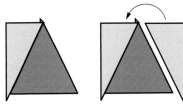

11. Place remaining Background triangle to the right of the Cone.

12. Flip right sides together, lining the top tip of both Background pieces together. Assembly-line sew.

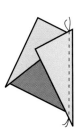

13. Set seams with Background on top, open, and press toward the Background fabric.

Squaring Up Cones

Patches are called Triangle in a Square Patches.
Patches for the Chain and Lattice quilts are
squared to 4½" with seam ¼" from top,
and ⅛" from bottom corners. Finished size
is 4" square.

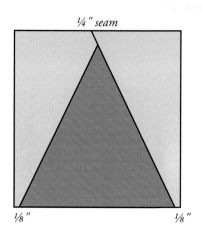

1. **Square Template:** Tape 4½" template to underneath corner of 6" x 6" ruler.

2. Place square ruler on patch. Line up turquoise lines with seams. Trim patch on two sides.

3. Turn patch. **Do not turn ruler.** Line up outside edges of template with cut edges. Trim patch on remaining two sides to 4½" square.

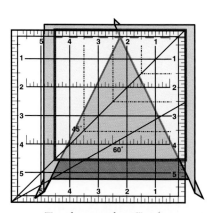

Template taped to 6" ruler

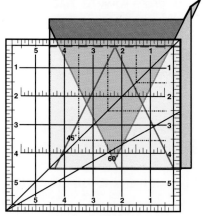

4. **Triangle in a Square Ruler:** Place patch on small cutting mat. Place square ruler on patch. Line turquoise lines on ruler with seams. Square up patch on all four sides to 4½" x 4½". Turn mat as you trim.

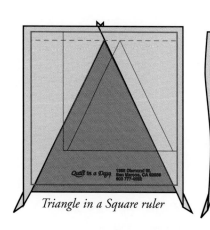

Triangle in a Square ruler

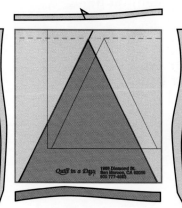

Completing the Cone Block

1. On each side of the Cone patch, sew 2½" x 4½" Background pieces. Clip connecting threads.

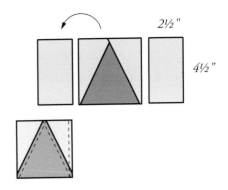

2. Press seams away from Cone. If necessary, sliver trim top edge to straighten.

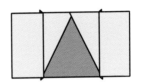 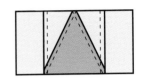

3. Sew 2½" x 8½" Background pieces to bottom of Cone and 4½" x 8½" Background pieces to top of Cone.

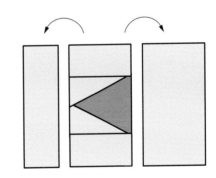

4. Press seams away from Cone. If necessary, sliver trim sides to straighten.

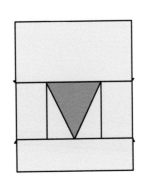 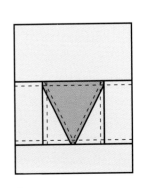

Making the Ice Cream Scoop

1. Find the large Ice Cream Scoop pattern on page 73. Trace on template plastic, and cut out.

2. Trace Scoop on **smooth side** of light weight non-woven fusible interfacing with permanent marking pen. Leave at least ½" between each shape.
   Chain Setting - trace 14
   Lattice and Cornerstone Setting - trace 10

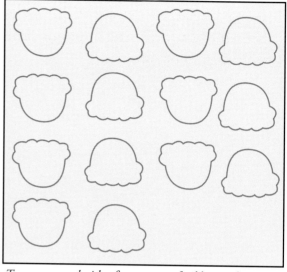

Trace on smooth side of non-woven fusible interfacing

3. Rough cut Scoops apart.
   Chain Setting - 7 pairs
   Lattice and Cornerstone Setting - 5 pairs

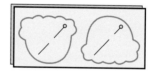

Non-woven fusible interfacing with pre-printed scoops is available from Quilt in a Day. This product saves the tracing step.

16

4. Place fusible side of Scoop shapes right sides together to the Ice Cream fabrics.

5. Using 18–20 stitches per inch, sew on drawn line. Use an open toe, metal applique foot, or plastic foot with metal bottom.

6. Trim to ⅛" from stitching line.

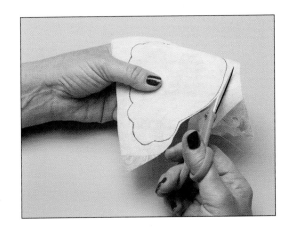

7. Clip inside curves to stitching at arrows.

8. Carefully cut a small slit in the middle of the fusible.

9. Cut a fat drinking straw in half. Insert straw into the slit. Push end of straw against the fabric. Stretch fabric over end of straw.

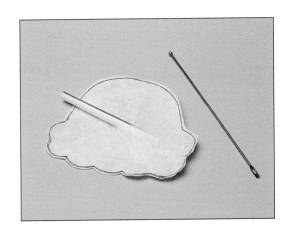

10. Place ball on ball point bodkin on fabric stretched over straw end. Gently push fabric into straw with the bodkin. This technique begins to turn the piece.

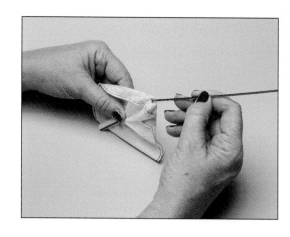

11. Remove the straw and bodkin. Finish turning with fingers.

12. Push out edges by running bodkin around the inside of the piece.

13. "Press" outside edges with a small wooden "pressing stick," or wooden iron. Press from inside of Scoop to outside, so fabric rolls over interfacing.

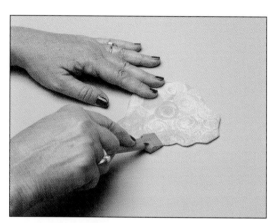

14. Place scoop on 100% cotton batting, and cut batting same size as scoop. Stuff using hemostats.

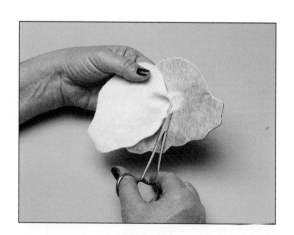

15. Fuse to top of Cone with hot steam iron.

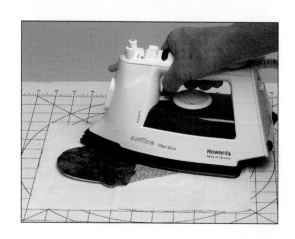

Applique the Scoop

1. Applique by hand or machine using a blind hem stitch or blanket stitch.

2. Sew a decorative stitch to enhance scoop shape.

Hand Applique

1. Thread #10 sharp or applique milliner's needle with 18" single strand of regular thread matching Ice Cream. Condition with Thread Heaven.

2. Bring thread up through Background and catch a couple of threads on fold of Ice Cream. Push needle down through Background right above spot where it came up.

3. Move needle ⅛" away, and come up through Background again. Pull stitches firmly but not tightly. If interfacing shows on edge, use tip of needle to tuck it under.

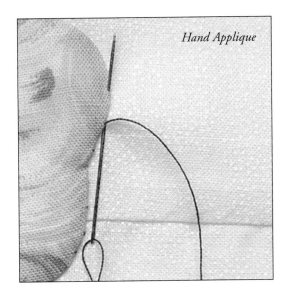

Hand Applique

Blind Hem Stitch by Machine

1. Set up machine with invisible thread on top. Loosen top tension. Use small, #70 needle.

2. Load bobbin with neutral thread to match Background. Set stitch length at 2.0 on computerized machines, or 15 stitches per inch, and stitch width at 1.5.

3. Position needle so straight stitches line up with the edge on the Background fabric and bite catches edge of applique. Stitch around Ice Cream, and lock ending stitches.

4. Use stiletto to roll under any exposed interfacing.

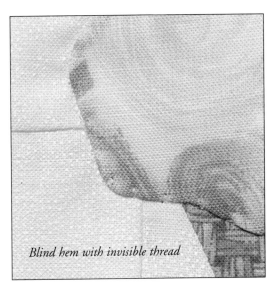

Blind hem with invisible thread

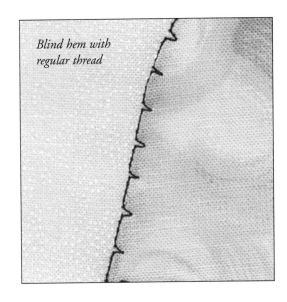

Blind hem with regular thread

Blanket Stitch by Machine

1. Select a coordinating or contrasting color for outlining. Use regular or heavy thread in the top, and regular matching thread in the bobbin. A suggested stitch length is 3.0 with a stitch width of 3.0.

2. Adjust stitch so that the straight stitch lines up with the Ice Cream on the Background, and the "bite" is into the applique. Stitch around Ice Cream, and lock ending stitches.

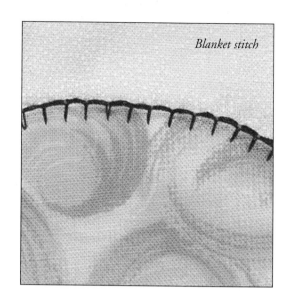

Blanket stitch

Decorative Stitch by Machine

1. The topstitch, or triple stitch, is perfect for enhancing the Ice Cream shape. This stitch is indicated on sewing machines with this symbol: ☰ ☰ ☰

2. The feather or herringbone stitch is another suggestion for enhancement.

3. Mark the curve with a hera marker or pencil, and stitch on the line.

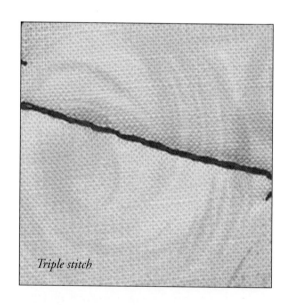

Triple stitch

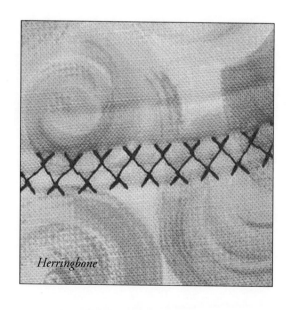

Herringbone

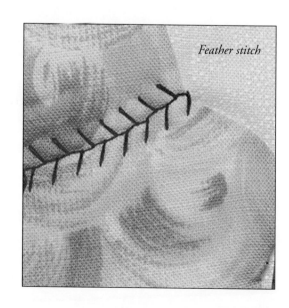

Feather stitch

Finishing the Chain Setting

Making the Chain Blocks

1. **Check your ¼" seam.** See page 8.

2. Cut Background and Chain strips in half.

3. Sew a 2" Chain half strip to each side of the 5½" Background half strip. Make three sets of half strips.

4. Set seams with Chain on top, open, and press toward Chain fabric. Patchwork should measure 8½" in width.

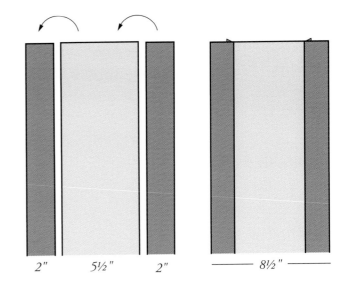

2"   5½"   2"   ——— 8½" ———

5. Cut into (24) 2" segments.

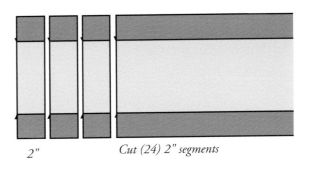

2"   *Cut (24) 2" segments*

6. Sew six pairs of 2" Chain half strips, and 2" Background half strips.

7. Set seams with Chain on top, open, and press toward Chain fabric.

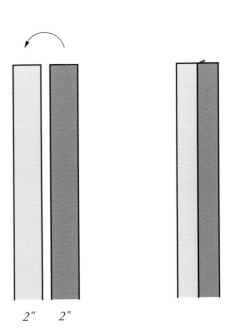

2"   2"

8. Sew six pairs with three 2½" Background half strips. Make three sets of half strips.

9. Press seams away from Background fabric. Patchwork should measure 8½" in width.

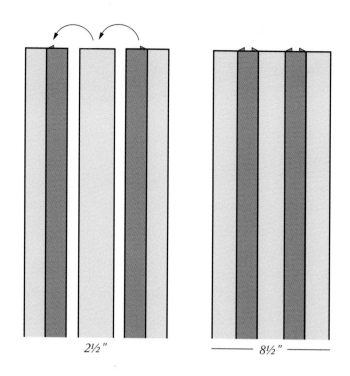

2½"

——— 8½" ———

10. Cut into (24) 2" segments.

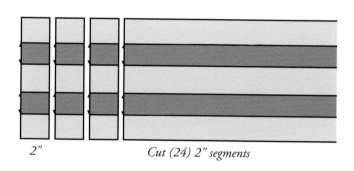

2"   *Cut (24) 2" segments*

11. Sew 3½" Background half strips to each side of 2½" Chain half strips. Make three sets of half strips.

12. Set seams with Chain on top, open and press toward Chain fabric. Patchwork should measure 8½" in width.

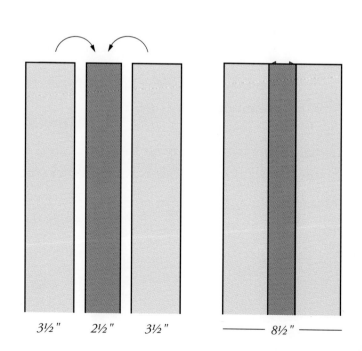

3½"   2½"   3½"

——— 8½" ———

13. Cut into (12) 4½" segments.

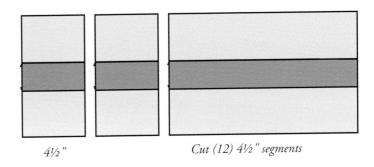

4½"   *Cut (12) 4½" segments*

14. Arrange segments in stacks of twelve.

15. Assembly-line sew together to complete the Chain block. Match and lock seams.

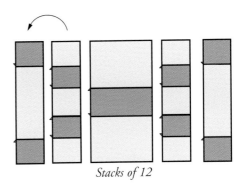

Stacks of 12

16. Press seams away from center row.

17. Compare the Ice Cream Cone Block with the Chain Block. Square the larger one to the same size as the smaller one. Trim equally on four sides.

Two blocks should be the same size

Sewing Top Together

1. Lay out Cone blocks and Chain blocks.

2. Flip second vertical row right sides together to first vertical row. Stack from bottom to top, so top blocks are on top of stack.

3. Assembly-line sew first two vertical rows together. Do not clip connecting threads.

4. Stack remaining rows from bottom to top.

5. Flip third vertical row right sides together to second row. Assembly-line sew.

6. Assembly-line sew remaining vertical rows.

7. Sew horizontal rows, pushing seams away from Chain blocks.

8. Press.

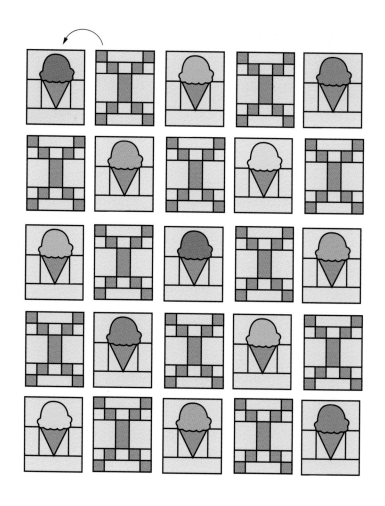

Adding the Framing Border

1. Trim selvages on 2" Framing Border strips, and piece three together into one long strip.

2. Measure sides. Cut two borders that measurement plus 1". Pin and sew to sides.

3. Press seams toward Framing Border. Trim ends even with quilt top.

4. Measure top and bottom, including side borders. Cut two borders that measurement plus 1". Pin and sew to top and bottom.

5. Press seams toward Framing Border. Trim ends.

Making the Rainbow Border

1. Sew the 2½" Ice Cream fabric strips together. Press seams to one side.

2. Cut into (17) 2½" segments.

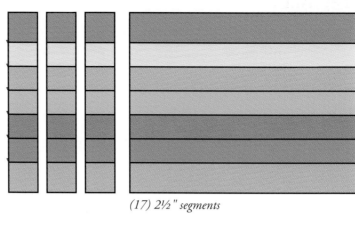

(17) 2½" segments

3. Sew the segments together end to end until you have enough for the sides, top and bottom borders. Keep all the seams going in the same direction.

4. Sew Rainbow Border to sides. Press seams toward Framing Border. Trim ends even with the quilt top.

5. Sew Rainbow Border to top and bottom. Press seams toward Framing Border. Trim ends even with the quilt top.

Layering

1. Tape or clamp the backing, right side down.

2. Spread batting on backing.

3. Spread quilt on top, right side up. Smooth until flat.

4. Safety pin layers together away from planned quilt lines.

Quilting Suggestions

1. Stitch down middle of Chain with walking foot.

2. Stitch in the Ditch around the Framing Border.

Mark center of Chain block from one corner to the other.

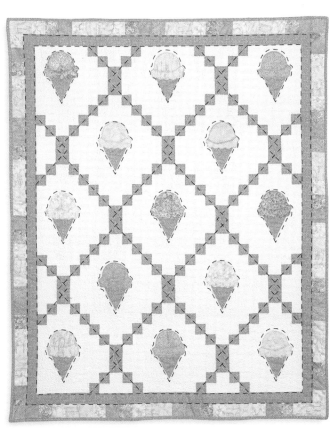

Mark center of Chain block from one corner to mid-way and then to opposite corner.

Free Motion Quilting with Darning Foot

1. Place a darning foot on sewing machine and drop or cover feed dogs with a plate. Use a fine needle and a little hole throat plate with a center needle position. Use invisible or regular thread in the top and regular thread to match the backing in the bobbin. Loosen the top tension if using invisible thread.

2. Bring the bobbin thread up ¼" from edge of Cone. Lower the needle into the background fabric and drop the foot. Moving the fabric very slowly, take a few tiny stitches to lock them. Snip off the tails of the threads.

3. With your eyes watching the outline of the Cone ahead of the needle, and your fingertips stretching the fabric and acting as a quilting hoop, move the fabric in a steady motion while the machine is running at a constant speed. Outline stitch around all Ice Cream Cones.

4. Lock off with tiny stitches and clip the threads at the end.

5. Free motion quilt around bottom edge of Ice Cream.

6. Stipple background by sewing a few stitches in one direction, then curve around and back toward the beginning making a loop.

7. Continue making loops without crossing previously sewn stippling until the background is filled.

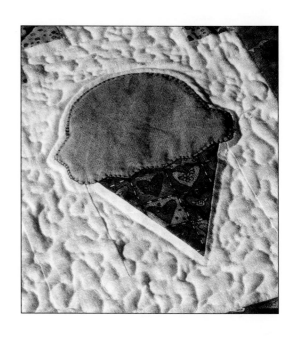

8. Move toward the edge, lock the stitches, and clip threads.

9. Binding instructions are on pages 70-71.

Finishing the Lattice and Cornerstones Quilt

Making the Cone Blocks

1. Make ten Cone blocks following directions on pages 12-15.

2. Make ten Ice Cream scoops following directions on pages 16-20, fuse to blocks, and stitch in place.

Making Lattice and Cornerstones

1. Cut the 1½" Lattice and Cornerstones strips in half.

2. Make three stacks of (14) 1½" half strips with Medium as first and last stacks, and Light in the middle.

3. Assembly-line sew Light strips to Medium strips.

4. Set seams with Medium on top, open, and press seams toward the Medium.

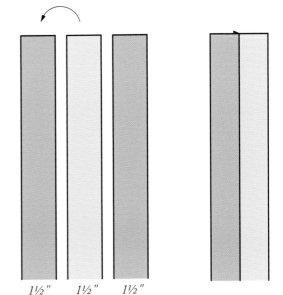

1½"   1½"   1½"

5. Sew remaining Medium strips to Light strips.

6. Press seams toward the Medium.

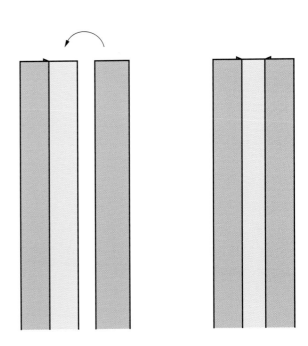

7. Measure the height and width of Cone Block. Record the measurements.

8. From each half strip, cut one Lattice the height and one the width.

9. Cut this many Lattice pieces.
    (12) pieces the height of your block approximately 10½"
    (12) pieces the width of your block approximately 8½"

10. Cut (16) 1½" pieces for Cornerstones.

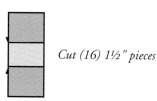

Cut (16) 1½" pieces

Making Sixteen Cornerstones

1. Make three stacks of (3) 1½" half strips with Light as first and last stacks and Medium in the middle.

2. Assembly-line sew Medium strips to Light strips.

3. Set seams with Medium on top, open, and press seams toward Medium.

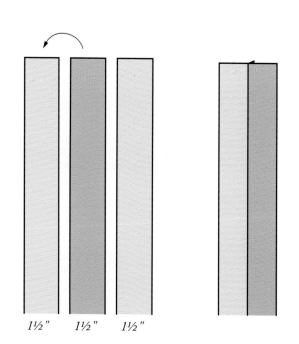

1½"   1½"   1½"

4. Sew remaining Light strips to Medium strips.

5. Press seams toward the Medium.

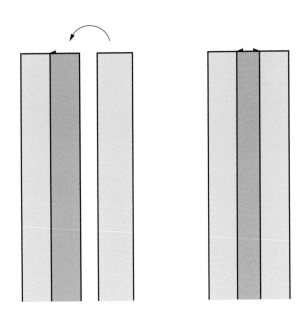

6. Cut (32) 1½" pieces.

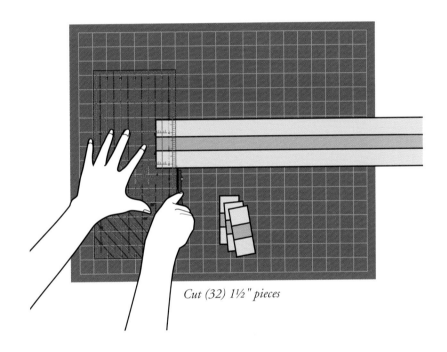

Cut (32) 1½" pieces

7. Make three stacks of (16) 1½" pieces.

8. Assembly-line sew middle stack to left stack. Do not clip connecting threads.

9. Assembly-line sew right stack to partially completed blocks. Clip connecting threads.

10. Press seams to the middle.

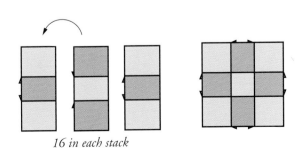

16 in each stack

Sewing the Top Together

1. Lay out (9) Ice Cream Cone Blocks, (12) 8½" Lattice, (12) 10½" Lattice and (16) Cornerstones.

2. Flip second vertical row right sides together to first vertical row. Stack from bottom to top, so first pair is on the top.

3. Stack remaining rows so top block is on the top.

4. Assembly-line sew vertical rows together. Do not clip connecting threads.

5. Sew horizontal rows together, locking seams, and pressing them away from the Lattice.

6. Press quilt top. Straighten outside edges.

Adding the Optional Border

1. Square selvage edges on 4½" Optional Border strips.

2. Piece three strips together into one long strip.

3. Measure sides. Cut two Borders same size.

4. Measure top and bottom. Cut two Borders same size.

5. Pin and sew Borders to sides. Press seams away from sides.

6. Sew 4½" squares to top and bottom borders.

7. Pin and sew to top and bottom.

Sue Bouchard   *44" x 50"*

Layering

1. Cut backing into two equal pieces, and sew together.

2. Tape or clamp the backing, right side down.

3. Spread batting on backing.

4. Spread quilt on top, right side up. Smooth until flat.

5. Safety pin layers together away from planned quilt lines.

Quilting Suggestions

1. Stitch in the Ditch along Lattice and Cornerstone seam lines to stabilize quilt.

2. Free motion machine quilt ¼" away from Cone.

3. Mark diagonal grid 1¼" apart on block background with hera marker. Machine quilt on lines with walking foot.

Triple Decker Wallhanging

Yardage

Background   ¼ yd

     (1) 7½" x 8½" piece
     (2) 3" x 6" pieces
     (2) 4½" x 2½" pieces
     (1) 2½" x 8½" piece

Cone   ¼ yd

     (1) 5" x 6" piece

3 different Ice Cream Fabrics   ¼ yd ea.

     (1) 5" x 6" piece of each

Narrow Border   ⅛ yd

     (2) 1¼" strips

Sue Bouchard   14" x 19"

Non-directional Border   ¼ yd

     (2) 3" strips

or

Directional Border   ½ yd

     (2) 3" x 16" (vertical)
     (2) 3" x 16" (horizontal)

Binding   ¼ yd

     (2) 3" strips

Batting (100% Cotton)   18" x 20"
    Stuffing for Scoops

Backing   ½ yd

Batting   18" x 22"

**Non-Woven
Fusible Interfacing**   5" x 22"

Making the Cone

1. Using the Triangle ruler, cut one Cone from the 5" x 6" piece.

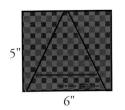 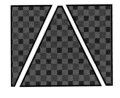

2. Layer **two** 3" x 6" Background rectangles wrong sides together. **This is essential for mirror imaging.**

3. Layer cut on one diagonal. Sort right side up. Eliminate two extra Background triangles.

 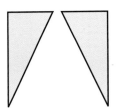

4. Lay out Cone with base at the bottom. Position Background triangles on each side of Cone.

5. Flip Cone right sides together to left Background triangle. Position Cone so Background fabric extends beyond Cone at top, creating a tip at the flat top.

 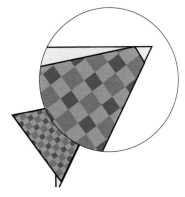

6. Sew with ¼" seam.

7. Press seam to Background.

8. Place remaining Background triangle to the right of the Cone. Flip right sides together, line the top tip of both pieces together, and sew.

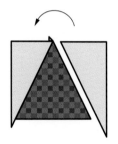

9. Press seam to Background.

10. Place on small cutting mat.

11. Line up turquoise triangle lines on Triangle in a Square ruler with seams. Trim on all four sides, squaring patch to 4½". Turn cutting mat as you trim.

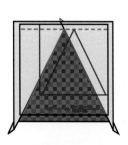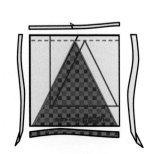

Making Three Ice Cream Scoops

1. Find the large Ice Cream Scoop
   pattern on page 73. Trace on
   template plastic, and cut out.

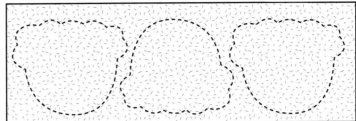

2. Trace three large Ice Cream Scoops
   onto the smooth side of the lightweight fusible interfacing.
   Leave ½" between Scoops. Rough-cut apart.

3. Place Scoop with fusible side of interfacing
   against right side of fabric.

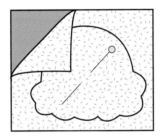 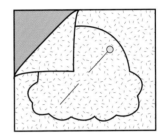 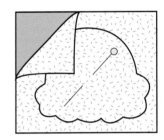

4. Sew on the lines with 20 stitches per inch.

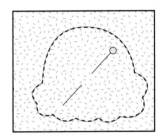

5. Trim to ⅛". Clip inside curves to stitching.

Clip to stitching

6. Cut a small slit in the middle of the fusible.
   Turn right side out.

7. Cut 100% cotton batting same size as Scoop
   and stuff with hemostats.

Completing the Block

1. Sew one 2½" x 4½" Background piece to each side of the Cone patch.

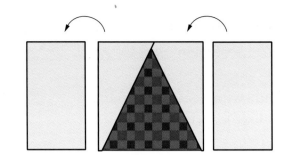

2. Press seams away from Cone.

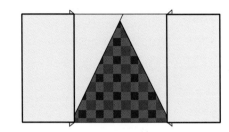

3. Sew the 7½" x 8½" Background piece to the top of the Cone.

4. Sew the 2½" x 8½" Background piece to the bottom of the Cone.

5. Press seams away from Cone.

6. If necessary, square sides.

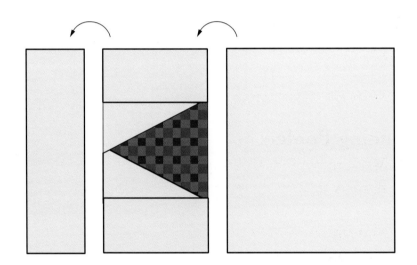

7. Position the three Scoops on the Cone, and fuse in place.

8. Applique around outside edges by machine or by hand. Sew a decorative stitch on top Scoop. See pages 19 – 20.

Sewing the Narrow Border

Sew 1¼" strips to Wallhanging as a Folded Border or regular Border.

1. **Folded Border:** With wrong sides together, press 1¼" strips in half lengthwise.

2. Match raw edges of Folded Border to raw edges of two opposite sides of Wallhanging.

3. Using 10 stitches per inch, sew with seam slightly less than ¼". Trim to match sides. Do not press out.

4. Sew Folded Border to top and bottom of Wallhanging, overlapping in corners.

Directional Border: Place strips beside patchwork and check before sewing.

Adding Borders and Finishing

1. Measure two sides. Cut, pin, and sew Borders to sides. Press seams toward Border.

2. Measure top and bottom. Cut, pin, and sew Borders to top and bottom. Press seams toward Border.

3. Machine quilt and bind.

Quilting Suggestions

1. Outline ¼" from Ice Cream Cone.

2. Stitch in the Ditch through the Folded Border.

3. Mark 1¼" grid on diagonal, and quilt with walking foot, or stipple Background with darning foot.

Pillow or Wallhanging

Yardage

Background ¼ yd

(2) 3" x 6" pieces
(2) 2½" x 4½" pieces
(1) 2½" x 8½" piece
(1) 4½" x 8½" piece

Cone ¼ yd

(1) 5" x 6" piece

Ice Cream ¼ yd

(1) 5" x 6" piece

6 different Scallop Fabrics ⅛ yd ea.

(1) 3" x 18" piece from each

First Border ⅛ yd

(1) 1½" strip

Border Sides ¼ yd

(2) 3½" strips

Border Corners ⅛ yd

(4) 3½" squares

Binding ¼ yd
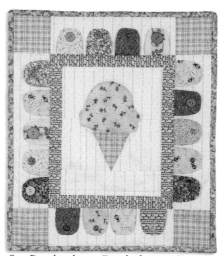
(2) 3" strips

Sue Bouchard   *Finished size 16" x 18"*

Backing ⅔ yd

Batting 20" x 22"

Non-Woven Fusible Interfacing ¼ yd

(1) 5" x 6" piece

Buttons

(18) from ⅜" to ¾"

Additional Supplies for Pillow

Pillow Backing ½ yd

(2) 12" x 20" pieces

Needle Punched Fleece ½ yd
(2) 15" x 17" pieces

Stuffing 12 oz. bag

Pillow or Wallhanging Instructions

1. Make one Ice Cream Cone block following directions on pages 12-20.

Making the Scallops

1. Fold six 3" x 18" Scallop fabrics in half with right sides together.

2. Use Scallop pattern to the right. Trace on template plastic, and cut out.

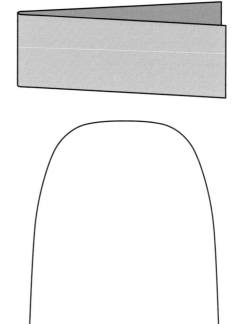

3. Trace three Scallop shapes on each of the six fabrics.

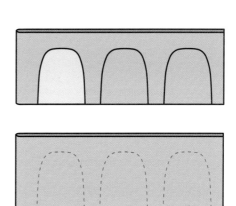

4. With 18-20 stitches per inch or a 1.5 setting on a computerized machine, sew on the drawn lines. Lock the stitches at the beginning and end of each Scallop.

5. Trim ⅛" from sewn line. Turn right side out.

6. Press with an iron.

Placing Scallops on Borders

1. Cut two 3½" x 12½" side Border strips and two 3½" x 10½" top and bottom Border strips. Fold in half and finger press. Use this as a reference point for placing Scallops.

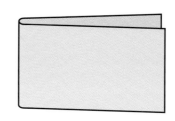 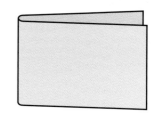

2. Starting from the middle of the strip, position Scallops. Place five Scallops on the sides and four Scallops on the top and bottom. Pin.

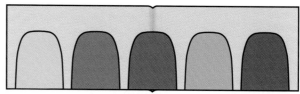

Border Sides

3. Baste in place ⅛" from the edge.

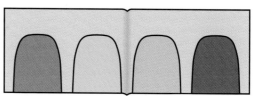

Border Top and Bottom

4. Add the Borders with Corners.

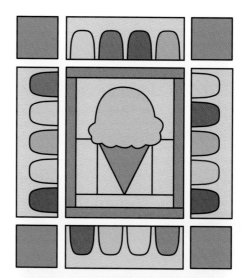

5. Layer top on 20" x 22" batting and backing, and safety pin.

6. Quilt ¼" around the Ice Cream Cone and along Borders.

7. Sew one button to each Scallop.

8. **Wallhanging only:** Add Binding. See pages 70 – 71.

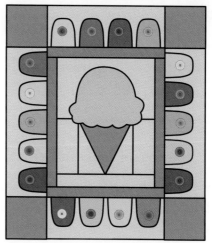

Completing the Pillow

1. Turn under one 20" side on each 12" x 20" pillow backing and hem.

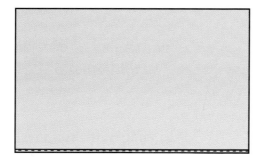 

2. Place the two pillow backs wrong side up and overlap them 4" in the center.

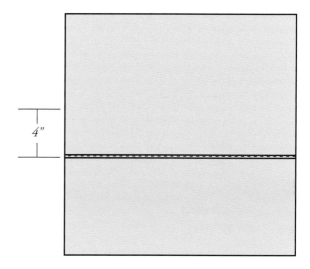

3. Center the Ice Cream Cone top on the backing. Pin outside edges together.

4. Add Binding. See pages 70 – 71.

5. **Pillow Form:** Stitch 15" x 17" needle punched fleece right sides together, leaving opening. Turn through opening.

6. Stuff, and sew opening closed.

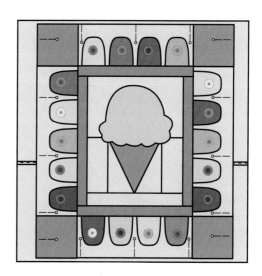

Happy Birthday Quilt

Yardage

Sue Bouchard   42" x 60"

Background for Total Quilt		2 yards
(Cut pieces for each row from this yardage.)		

Letters and Candles — Row 1 and 5

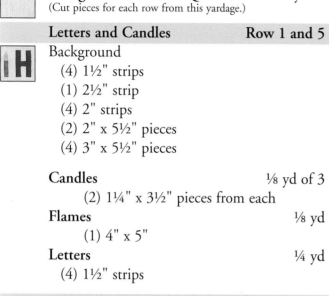

Background
- (4) 1½" strips
- (1) 2½" strip
- (4) 2" strips
- (2) 2" x 5½" pieces
- (4) 3" x 5½" pieces

Candles   ⅛ yd of 3
- (2) 1¼" x 3½" pieces from each

Flames   ⅛ yd
- (1) 4" x 5"

Letters   ¼ yd
- (4) 1½" strips

Hats — Row 2

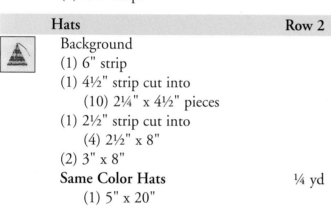

Background
- (1) 6" strip
- (1) 4½" strip cut into
  - (10) 2¼" x 4½" pieces
- (1) 2½" strip cut into
  - (4) 2½" x 8"
- (2) 3" x 8"

Same Color Hats   ¼ yd
- (1) 5" x 20"

Different Color Hats   ¼ yd of 5
- (1) 5" x 6" from each

⅛" Ribbons   ½ yd of 6

Sundaes — Row 3

Background
- (1) 11" strip cut into
  - (3) 11" x 12"

Bowls   ¼ yd
- (1) 7" x 12"

Bananas   ¼ yd
- (1) 8" x 7"

Ice Cream Scoops   ¼ yd of 3
- (1) 5" x 6" from each

Topping   ⅛ yd
- (1) 3½" x 7"

Cherries
- (3) Red Buttons

Ice Cream Cones — Row 4

Background
- (1) 7" strip cut into
  - (6) 7" x 4" pieces
  - (6) 7" x 2½" pieces
- (1) 5" strip
- (1) 2¼" strip cut into
  - (12) 2¼" x 3½" pieces

Cones   ⅛ yd
- (1) 4" x 21"

Ice Cream   ⅛ yd of 6
- (1) 4" x 5" from each

Non Directional Lattice and Borders   1½ yds
- (4) 2½" strips
- (5) 5" strips

Directional Lattice and Borders   2½ yds
- (4) 2½" strips
- (3) 5" strips cut selvage to selvage
- (2) 5" x 54" strips cut lengthwise

Non-Woven Fusible Interfacing   ¾ yd

Backing   3 yds

Batting   50" x 76"

Binding   ⅝ yd
- (6) 3" strips

Making Six Cones

Make six cones - five for the quilt, and one for the label.

1. Fold the 5" Background strip in half wrong sides together. **This step is essential for mirror images pieces.**

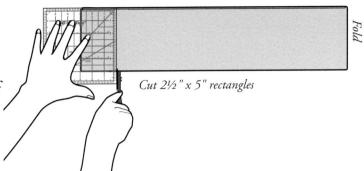

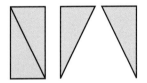

Cut 2½" x 5" rectangles

2. With 6" square ruler, layer cut three pairs of 2½" x 5" rectangles, for a total of six 2½" x 5" rectangles.

3. Layer cut each set of rectangles on one diagonal. Sort the triangles so they are right sides up.

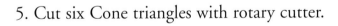

4. Place 4" Cone strip right side up.
   Triangle Template: Trace six triangles on strip.
   Triangle Ruler: Place Triangle ruler on strip, accurately lining up the narrow part of the triangle with the top of the strip. Line up the red line with the bottom of the strip.

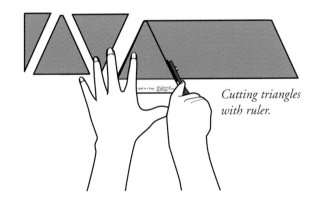

Cutting triangles with ruler.

5. Cut six Cone triangles with rotary cutter.

6. Lay out Cone with the base at the bottom. Position Background triangles on each side of Cone. Make sure all fabrics are turned right side up.

7. Set the right Background triangle aside. Flip Cone triangle right sides together to left Background triangle.

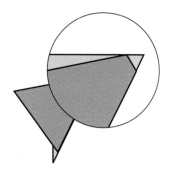

8. Position the triangles so Background fabric extends beyond Cone fabric at the top, creating a tip at the flat top.

9. Assembly-line sew with an accurate ¼" seam. Use stiletto to guide pieces.

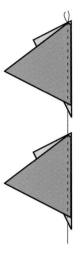

10. Set seams with Background on top, open, and press toward Background fabric.

11. Place remaining Background triangle to the right of the Cone.

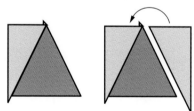

12. Flip right sides together, lining the top tip of both Background pieces together. Assembly-line sew.

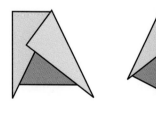

13. Set seams with Background on top, open, and press toward the Background fabric.

Squaring Up Cones

Cones for the Birthday Quilt are squared to 3½"
with seam ¼" from top, and ⅛" from corners.
Finished size is 3".

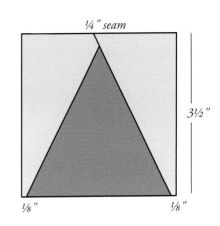

Square Template

See Pages 7 and 14. Line up red triangle lines
with seams. Trim patch on two sides. Turn patch.
Line up red lines with cut edges. Trim on remaining sides to 3½".

Triangle in a Square Ruler

1. Place square ruler on patch. Line up **red lines**
   with seams. Trim patch on two sides.

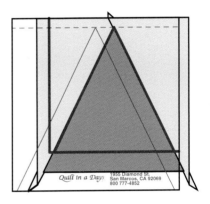

2. Turn patch. **Do not turn ruler.** Line up red
   square lines with cut edges. Trim patch on
   remaining two sides to 3½" square.

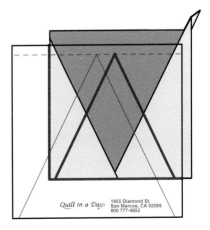

Completing the Cone Block

1. On each side of the Cone patch, sew 2¼" x 3½" Background pieces.

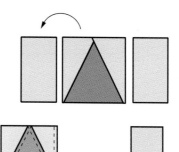

2. Press seams away from Cone. If necessary, sliver trim edges.

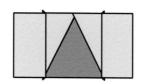 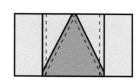

3. Sew 2½" x 7" Background pieces to bottom of Cone and 4" x 7" Background pieces to top of Cone.

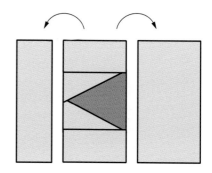

4. Press seams on two blocks toward the Cone, and seams on four blocks away from the Cone.

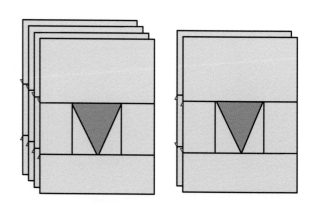

Making the Six Ice Cream Scoops

1. Find the small Ice Cream Scoop on page 73. Trace on template plastic, and cut out.

2. Trace six small Scoops on **smooth side** of light weight non-woven fusible interfacing with permanent marking pen. Leave at least ½" between each shape.

3. Rough cut Scoops apart.

4. Place fusible side of Scoop shapes right sides together to the Ice Cream fabrics.

5. Using 18–20 stitches per inch, sew on drawn line.

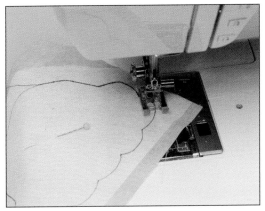

Sew on the line.

6. Trim to ⅛" from stitching line.

7. Clip inside curves to stitching.

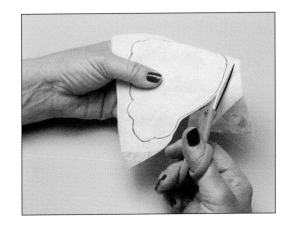

8. Carefully cut a small slit in the middle of the fusible.

9. Cut a fat drinking straw in half. Insert straw into the slit. Push end of straw against the fabric. Stretch fabric over end of straw.

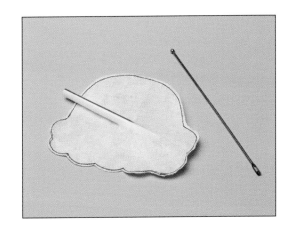

10. Place ball of ball point bodkin on fabric stretched over straw end. Gently push fabric into straw with the bodkin. This technique begins to turn the piece.

11. Remove the straw and bodkin. Finish turning with fingers.

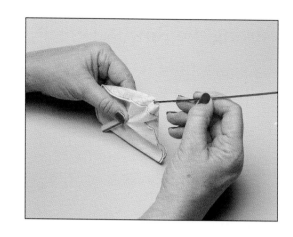

12. Push out edges by running bodkin around the inside of the piece.

13. "Press" outside edges with a small wooden "pressing stick," or wooden iron.

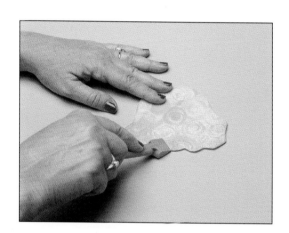

14. Place Scoop on 100% cotton batting, and cut batting same size as Scoop. Stuff using hemostats.

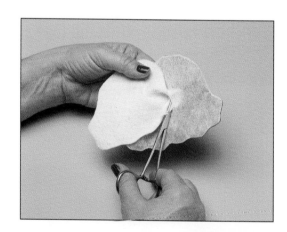

15. Fuse to top of Cone with hot steam iron.

16. Applique using a blind hem stitch or blanket stitch by hand or machine. Sew a decorative stitch to enhance Scoop shape. See pages 19-20.

17. Set one Ice Cream Cone aside for the label.

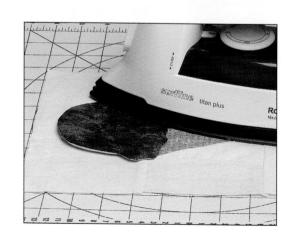

Sewing the Row Together

1. Lay out the five Cone blocks, alternating the seams.

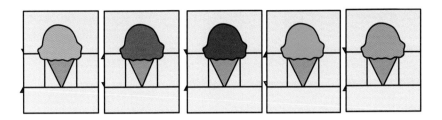

2. Sew the row together, locking seams.

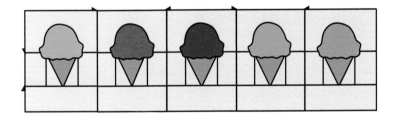

3. Trim row to 32½".

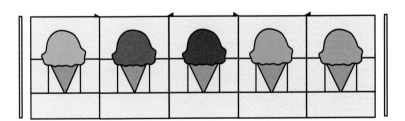

Making the Hat Row

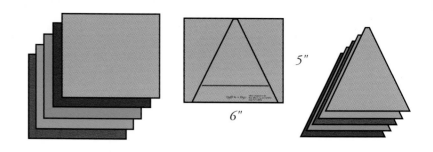

1. Using the Triangle ruler, cut five Hats from the 5" x 6" Hat fabric.

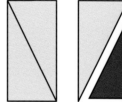

2. Fold 6" Background strip in half wrong sides together. Layer cut three pairs of 3" x 6" rectangles. Layer cut on one diagonal. Stack so they are right side up with Hats.

3. Sew five Hats.

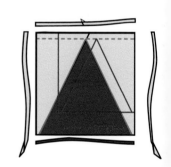

4. Place patch on small cutting mat.

5. Line up turquoise triangle lines on seams, and square to 4½".

6. Cut ribbon into fifteen 4" pieces.

7. Baste three ribbons at top of Hat ⅛" from edge.

8. Sew 2¼" x 4½" Background pieces to top and bottom of Hat.

9. Press top Background piece toward Hat so the ribbons stand up. Press bottom Background piece away from Hat.

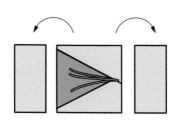
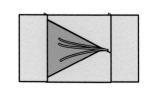

10. Sew the (4) 2½" x 8" Background pieces between each Hat and the 3" x 8" Background pieces on each end.

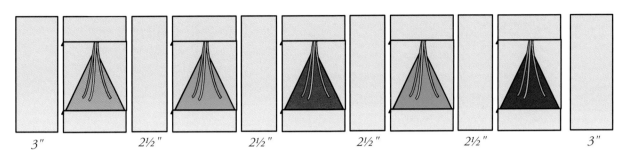

11. Press seams away from Hat blocks.

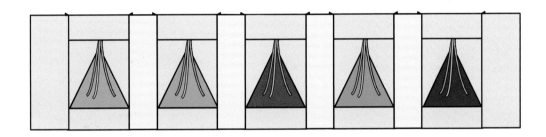

12. Trim row to 32½".

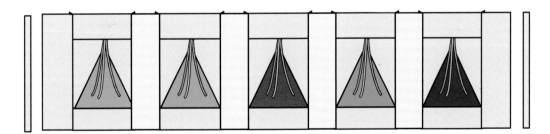

Making the Sundae Row

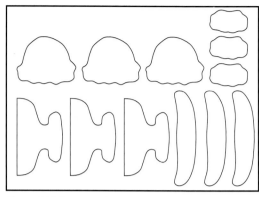

1. Find Sundae patterns on page 73. Trace on template plastic and cut out.

2. Trace three Bowls, three Bananas, three large Ice Cream Scoops and three Toppings on the smooth side of the lightweight fusible interfacing. **Leave ½" between shapes.**

Leave ½ " between shapes.

3. Sew on the lines with 18-20 stitches per inch, trim ⅛" from stitching. Clip inside curves and turn right side out.

Turning the Banana

1. Cut a small hole in the center of the interfacing.

2. Insert straw and turn first half with bodkin.

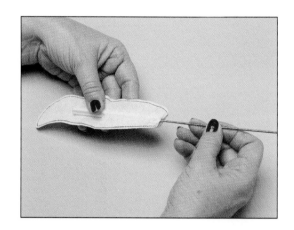

3. Insert straw in remaining half, and turn right side out.

Finishing the Block

1. Fold each 11" x 12" Background rectangle in half at 6". Finger press to mark the middle.

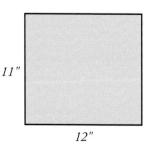

11"

12"

11"

6"

2. Fold Bananas in half and finger press.

3. Line up the middle of the Banana to the middle of the Background rectangle 3½" from the bottom. Fuse into place and applique.

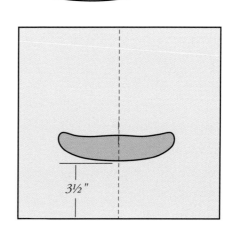

3½"

4. Using the Placement sheet for the Sundae, position the Bowl, Ice Cream and Topping in place. Fuse to the Background and Banana. Applique in place.

5. Square one to 10½" x 11". Square two to 10½" x 12". Trim equally from top and bottom.

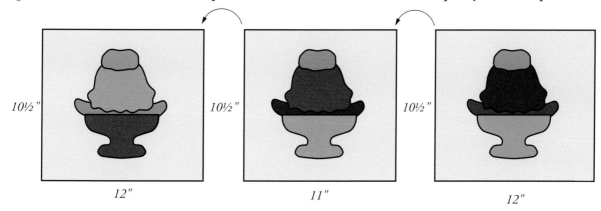

10½"   10½"   10½"

12"   11"   12"

6. Sew the Sundae blocks together.

7. Trim row to 32½".

Making Six Candles

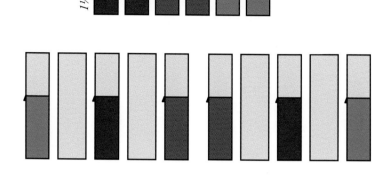

1. From 2½" Background strip, cut six 1¼" x 2½" pieces. From the 1½" strip, cut four 1½" x 5½" pieces .

2. Assembly-line sew 1¼" x 2½" Background pieces to 1¼" x 3½" Candle pieces.

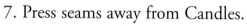

3. Press seams toward Candles. Clip apart.

4. Lay out Candles to make sure they are in the right order. Place a 1½" x 5½" Background strip between each Candle.

5. Sew Candles together. Press seams toward the 1½" x 5½" Background strips.

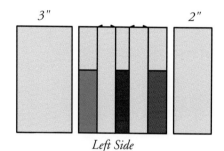

Left Side

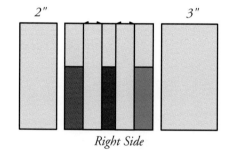

Right Side

6. Sew 2" x 5½" Background pieces to the inside Candles and 3" x 5½" Background pieces to the outside Candles.

7. Press seams away from Candles.

Making the Flames

1. Trace six Flames on the smooth side of the non-woven fusible interfacing. Flame pattern on page 73.

2. Place fusible side of interfacing against right side of fabric.

3. Sew on the lines, trim ⅛" from lines, and turn right side out.

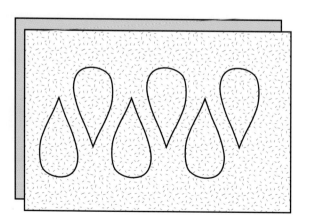

4. Fuse to the tops of the Candles.

5. Applique by hand or by machine.

Making the Happy Birthday Letters

1. From four 1½" Background strips cut:
    (11) 1½" x 5½"
    (2) 1½" x 4½"
    (1) 1½" x 3½"
    (12) 1½" x 2½"
    (11) 1½" squares

2. From one 2½" Background strip cut:
    (3) 2½" squares

3. From four 1½" Letter strips cut:
    (16) 1½" x 5½"
    (1) 1½" x 4½"
    (1) 1½" x 4"
    (6) 1½" x 3½"
    (6) 1½" x 2½"
    (17) 1½" squares

4. Follow the sewing illustrations to complete the Happy Birthday Letters. **Sew with a scant ¼" seam. On sewing machines with multiple needle positions achieve a scant ¼" by by moving the needle one position to the right.**

5. Press seams toward the Letter fabric.

6. Make two 'H' letters.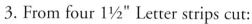

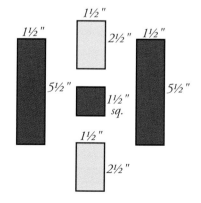

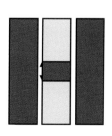

3½" x 5½"
3" x 5" finished

7. Make two 'A' letters.

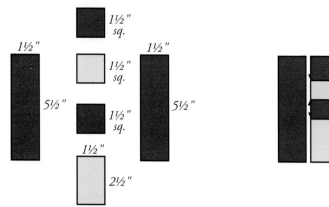
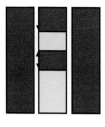
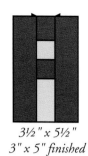

3½" x 5½"
3" x 5" finished

8. Make two 'P' letters.

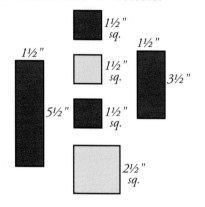
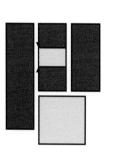
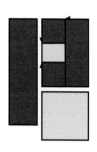
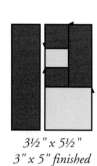

3½" x 5½"
3" x 5" finished

9. Make two 'Y' letters.

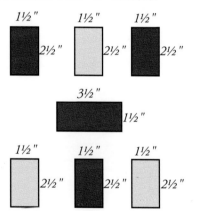
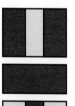

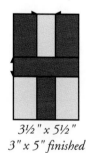

3½" x 5½"
3" x 5" finished

10. Make one 'B' letter.

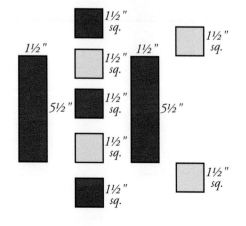
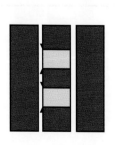
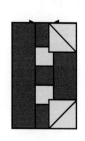

3½" x 5½"
3" x 5" finished

11. No piecing is required for the 'I' letter. ——————————

1½"

5½"

1" x 5" finished

12. Make one 'R' letter. ——————————

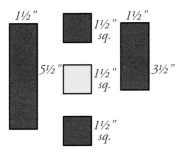

1½" *1½" sq.* *1½"*

5½" *1½" sq.* *3½"*

1½" sq.

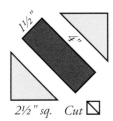

1½" *4"*

2½" sq.   Cut ◻

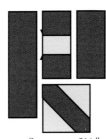

Square to 2½"

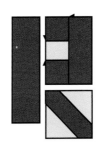

3½" x 5½"
3" x 5" finished

13. Make one 'T' letter. ——————————

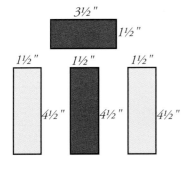

3½"
1½"

1½" *1½"* *1½"*

4½" *4½"* *4½"*

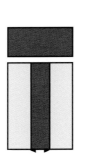

3½" x 5½"
3" x 5" finished

14. Make one 'D' letter. ——————————

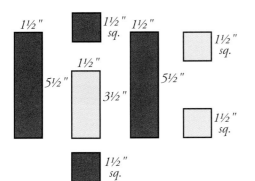

1½" *1½" sq.* *1½"*

5½" *1½"* *5½"* *1½" sq.*

3½"

1½" sq.

1½" sq.

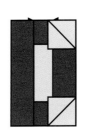

3½" x 5½"
3" x 5" finished

Sewing the Letters Together

1. Lay out your letters to make sure they are in the right order. Place a 1½" x 5½" Background strip between each letter.

2. Sew the Letters together.

3. Press the seams toward the 1½" x 5½" Background strips.

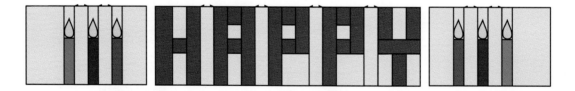

Completing Rows One and Five

1. Sew Candle sections to both sides of "HAPPY". Place 3" x 5½" Background pieces at ends of row. Press seams toward Candles.

2. Sew one 3" x 5½" Background piece to each end of "BIRTHDAY". Press seams away from Letters.

3. Sew 2" Background strips to top and bottom of letter rows. Press seams away from Letters.

4. Trim rows to 32½".

Finishing the Quilt

1. Trim four 2½" Lattice strips to 32½" in length.

2. Lay out the rows with the Lattice strips and sew together.

3. Press seams toward Lattice.

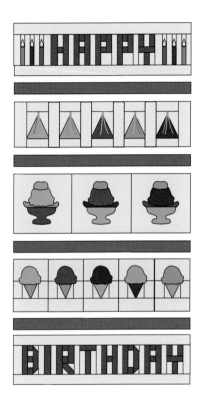

4. Sew 5" Side Borders to quilt top. Press seams toward Borders.

5. Sew 5" Top and Bottom Borders to quilt. Press seams toward Borders.

6. Sew cherry buttons to top of sundaes.

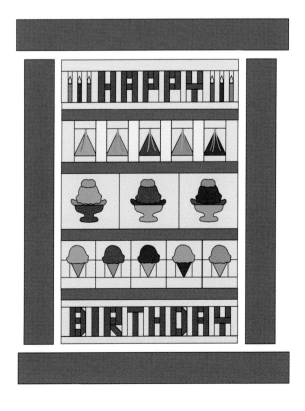

Personalizing the Happy Birthday Quilt

Personalize your quilt by adding the quilt recipient's name. The name becomes the "sixth row" placed right below "Birthday".

1. Locate additional letters other than "HAPPY BIRTHDAY" on pages 63 – 67. Seven letters is the maximum number. If the name is too long, use a shorter nickname.

2. Sew letters.

3. Cut 1½" x 5½" Background strips for spacers between each letter.

4. Sew letters together with Background strips. Press seams toward Background strips. Measure length of sewn together letters.

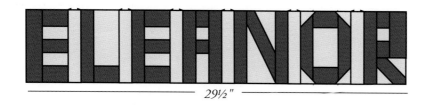

29½"

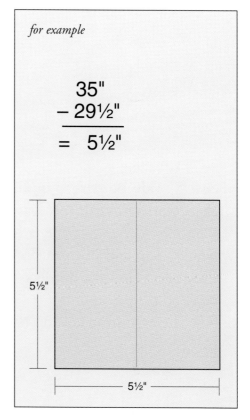

for example

$$35"$$
$$- 29½"$$
$$= 5½"$$

5½"

5½"

5. Subtract length of letters from 35". Cut a piece of Background fabric that measurement x 5½".

6. Cut Background piece in half, and sew half to each end of row.

7. Cut two 2" strips selvage to selvage from Background fabric.

8. Sew 2" strips to top and bottom of Personalized Name row. Press seams toward Background strips.

9. Trim row to 32½".

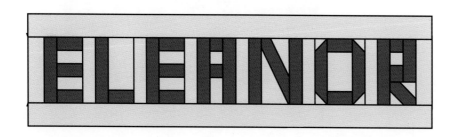

How to Make the Remainder of the Alphabet

Sew with a scant ¼" seam. Press seams toward the Letter fabric.

Letter C

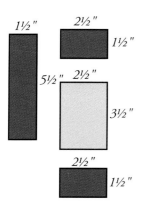
1½"   2½"   1½"
5½"   2½"   3½"
2½"   1½"

3½" x 5½"
3" x 5" finished

Letter E

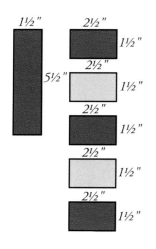
1½"   2½"   1½"
5½"   2½"   1½"
2½"   1½"
2½"   1½"
2½"   1½"

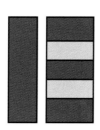

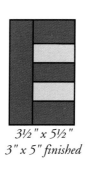
3½" x 5½"
3" x 5" finished

Letter F

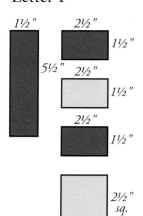
1½"   2½"   1½"
5½"   2½"   1½"
2½"   1½"
2½" sq.

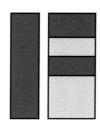

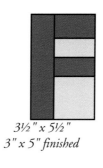
3½" x 5½"
3" x 5" finished

Letter G

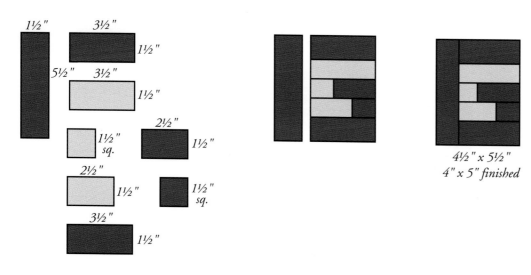

1½"   3½"
1½"
5½"   3½"
1½"
1½" sq.   2½"
1½"
2½"
1½"   1½" sq.
3½"
1½"

4½" x 5½"
4" x 5" finished

Letter J

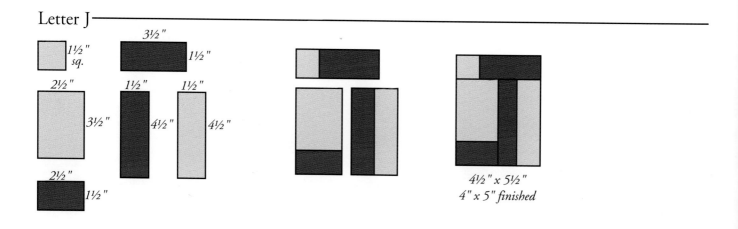

1½" sq.
3½"
1½"
2½"   1½"   1½"
3½"   4½"   4½"
2½"
1½"

4½" x 5½"
4" x 5" finished

Letter K

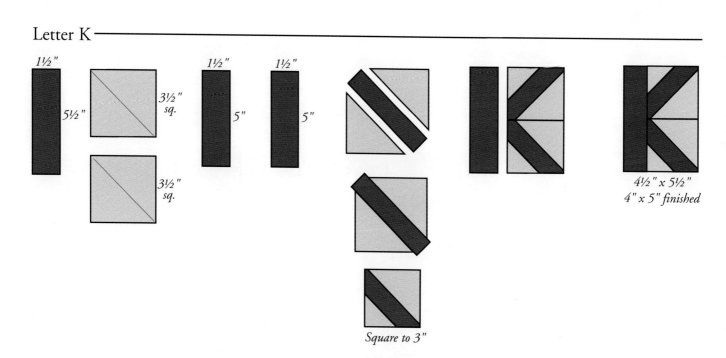

1½"   1½"   1½"
5½"   3½" sq.   5"   5"
3½" sq.

4½" x 5½"
4" x 5" finished

Square to 3"

Letter L

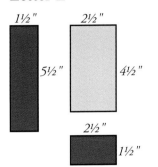
1½" 2½"
5½" 4½"
2½"
1½"

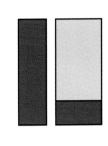

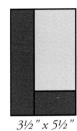

3½" x 5½"
3" x 5" finished

Letter M or W

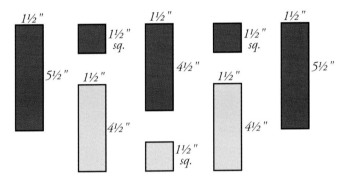
1½" 1½" sq. 1½" 1½" sq. 1½"
5½" 1½" 4½" 1½" 5½"
4½" 1½" sq. 4½"

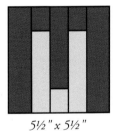

5½" x 5½"
5" x 5" finished

5½" x 5½"
5" x 5" finished

Letter N

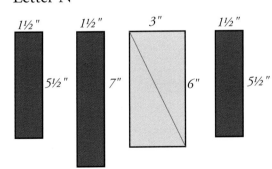
1½" 1½" 3" 1½"
5½" 7" 6" 5½"

4½" x 5½"
4" x 5" finished

Square to
2½" x 5½"

Letter O and Q

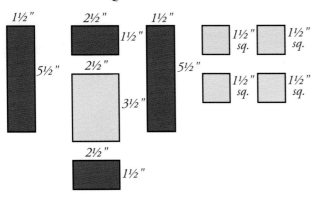

1½" 2½" 1½"
1½"
5½" 2½" 5½"
3½"
2½"
1½"

1½" sq. 1½" sq.
1½" sq. 1½" sq.

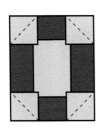  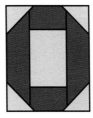  

4½" x 5½"
4" x 5" finished

4½" x 5½"
4" x 5" finished

Q only
See flame
page 56

Letter S

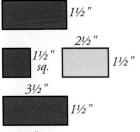

3½"
1½"
1½" sq. 2½" 1½"
3½"
1½"
2½" 1½"
1½" sq.
3½"
1½"

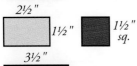

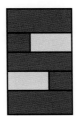

3½" x 5½"
3" x 5" finished

Letter U

1½" 1½" 1½"
5½" 4½" 5½"
1½" sq.

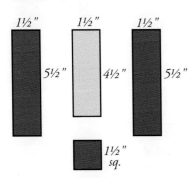

3½" x 5½"
3" x 5" finished

Letter V

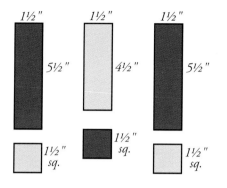

1½"
5½"
1½"
4½"
1½"
5½"

1½" sq.
1½" sq.
1½" sq.

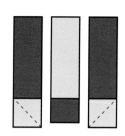

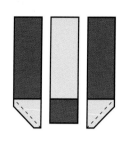

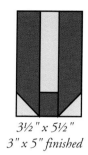

3½" x 5½"
3" x 5" finished

Letter X

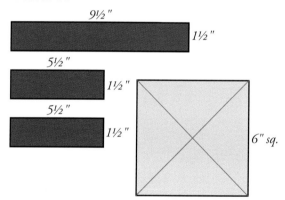

9½"
1½"
5½"
1½"
5½"
1½"
6" sq.

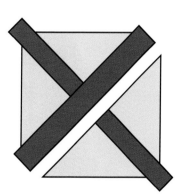

5½" x 5½"
5" x 5" finished

Letter Z

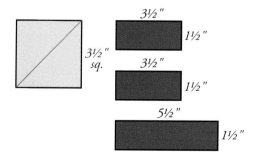

3½" sq.
3½"
1½"
3½"
1½"
5½"
1½"

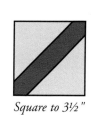

Square to 3½"

3½" x 5½"
3" x 5" finished

Finishing the Quilt

1. Cut the backing yardage in two equal pieces.

2. Sew the backing pieces together to make a backing larger than the quilt top.

3. Spread out the backing on a large table or floor area with the right side down. Clamp the fabric to the edge of the table with quilt clips or tape the backing to the floor. Do not stretch the backing.

4. Layer the batting on top of the backing, and pat flat.

5. With the quilt top right side up, center on the backing. Smooth until all layers are flat. Clamp or tape outside edges.

6. Safety pin the layers together every three to five inches. Pin next to your machine quilting lines.

"Stitch in the Ditch" to Anchor the Rows and Borders

1. Attach your walking foot, and lengthen the stitch to 8 to 10 stitches per inch or 3.5 on computerized machines.

2. Roll to the center row. Clip the rolls in place.

3. Spread the seams open, and "stitch in the ditch."

4. Unroll the quilt to the next seam. Clip the roll in place, and "stitch in the ditch."

5. Continue to unroll and roll the quilt until all the seams are stitched, anchoring the blocks.

6. Stitch in the ditch on the border seams.

The ideal machine quilting area is a sewing machine bed level with the table, and a large area to the left of the machine to support the quilt. Machine quilt on a day when you are relaxed to help avoid muscle strain down your neck, shoulders, and back. Sit in a raised stenographer's chair so your arms can rest on the table.

Free Motion Stitch Around Pieces

1. Drop your feed dogs, attach your darning foot and thread your machine with matching thread or invisible thread. If you use invisible thread, loosen your top tension. Match the bobbin thread to the backing.

2. Free motion sew around each of the Hats, Cones, Letters, Candles, and Sundaes.

Adding the Binding

Use a walking foot attachment and regular thread on top and in the bobbin to match the binding.

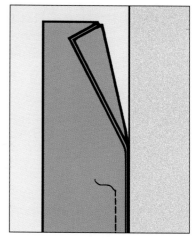

1. Square off the selvage edges, and sew 3" strips together lengthwise.

2. Fold and press in half with wrong sides together.

3. Line up the raw edges of the folded binding with the raw edges of the quilt in the middle of one side.

4. Begin stitching 4" from the end of the binding. Sew with 10 stitches per inch, or 3.0 to 3.5.

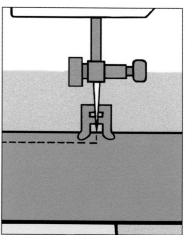

5. At the corner, stop the stitching ¼" from the edge with the needle in the fabric. Raise the presser foot and turn the quilt to the next side. Put the foot back down.

6. Stitch backwards ¼" to the edge of the binding, raise the foot, and pull the quilt forward slightly.

7. Fold the binding strip straight up on the diagonal. Fingerpress the diagonal fold.

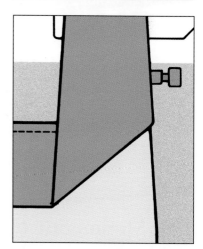

8. Fold the binding strip straight down with the diagonal fold underneath. Line up the top of the fold with the raw edge of the binding underneath.

9. Begin sewing from the edge.

10. Continue stitching and mitering the corners around the outside of the quilt.

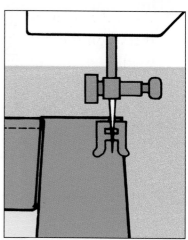

11. Stop stitching 4" from where the ends will overlap.

12. Line up the two ends of binding. Trim the excess with a ½" overlap.

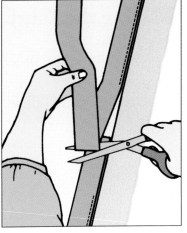

13. Open out the folded ends and pin right sides together. Sew a ¼" seam.

14. Continue to stitch the binding in place.

15. Trim the batting and backing up to the raw edges of the binding.

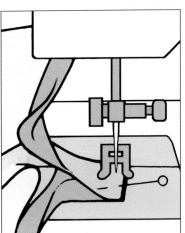

16. Fold the binding to the back side of the quilt. Pin in place so that the folded edge on the binding covers the stitching line. Tuck in the excess fabric at each miter on the diagonal.

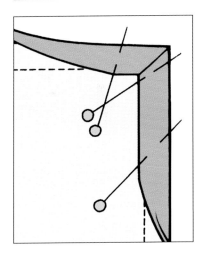

17. From the right side, "stitch in the ditch" using invisible thread on the front side, and a bobbin thread to match the binding on the back side. Catch the folded edge of the binding on the back side with the stitching.
Optional: Hand stitch binding in place.

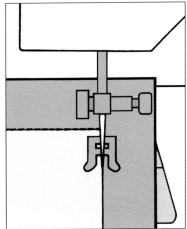

Making the Label

Use the extra Ice Cream Cone block made for the label.

1. Turn under the outside raw edges. Edgestitch in place.

2. With a fine point, permanent marking pen, write this information on the block:
   - who the quilt is for
   - the date
   - what event the quilt was made for
   - name of quiltmaker

3. Heat set the writing with a hot iron so the documentation will not fade with time.

4. Hand whip stitch the label to the back side, in the bottom right corner of the quilt.

This is the label for the back of Eleanor's Birthday Quilt. Remember, the quilt is never done until there is a label on the back!

Patterns

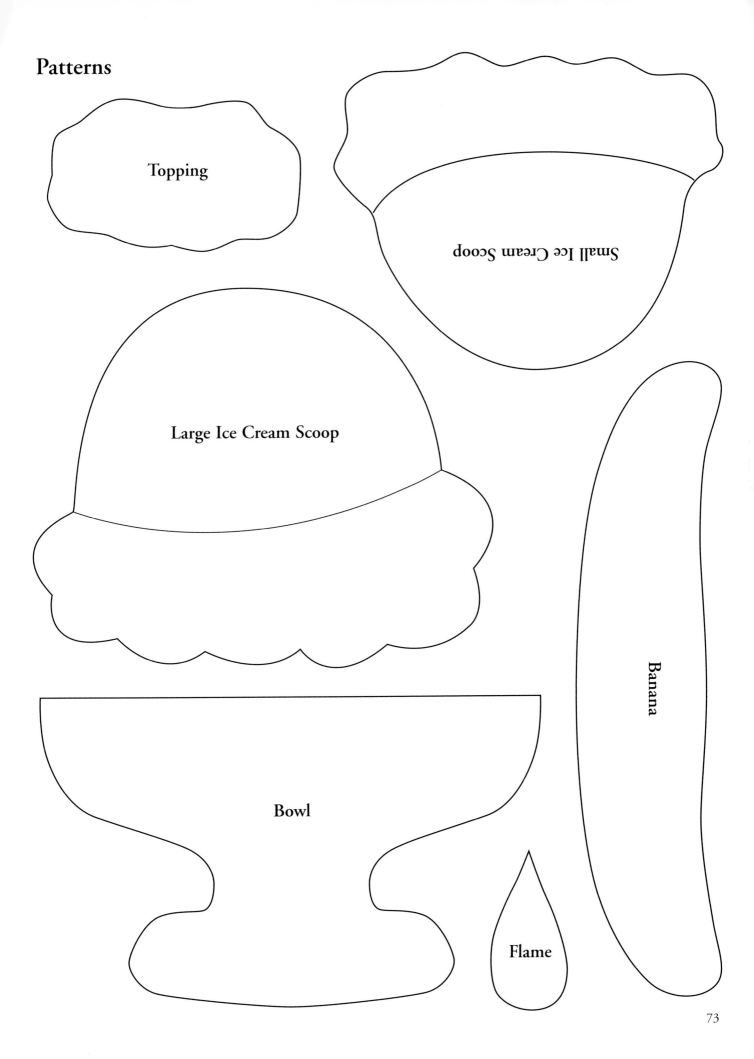

Topping

Small Ice Cream Scoop

Large Ice Cream Scoop

Banana

Bowl

Flame

Sundae Placement Sheet

Index

Order Information

Quilt in a Day books offer a wide range of techniques and are directed toward a variety of skill levels. If you do not have a quilt shop in your area, you may write or call for a complete catalog and current price list of all books and patterns published by Quilt in a Day®, Inc.

Easy

Make a Quilt in a Day Log Cabin
Irish Chain in a Day
Bits & Pieces Quilt
Trip Around the World Quilt
Heart's Delight Wallhanging
Scrap Quilt, Strips and Spider Webs
Rail Fence Quilt
Flying Geese Quilt
Star for all Seasons Placemats
Winning Hand Quilt
Courthouse Steps Quilt
Nana's Garden Quilt
Double Pinwheel
Easy Strip Tulip
Northern Star

Applique

Applique in a Day
Dresden Plate Quilt
Sunbonnet Sue Visits Quilt in a Day
Recycled Treasures
Country Cottages and More
Creating with Color
Spools & Tools Wallhanging
Dutch Windmills Quilt
Grandmother's Garden Quilt

Intermediate

Trio of Treasured Quilts
Lover's Knot Quilt
Amish Quilt
May Basket Quilt
Morning Star Quilt
Friendship Quilt
Kaleidoscope Quilt
Machine Quilting Primer
Star Log Cabin Quilt

Burgoyne Surrounded Quilt
Snowball Quilt
Tulip Table Runner
Jewel Box
Triple Irish Chain Quilts
Bears in the Woods

Holiday

Christmas Quilts and Crafts
Country Christmas
Bunnies & Blossoms
Patchwork Santa
Last Minute Gifts
Angel of Antiquity
Log Cabin Wreath Wallhanging
Log Cabin Christmas Tree Wallhanging
Country Flag
Lover's Knot Placemats
Stockings & Small Quilts

Sampler

The Sampler
Block Party Series 1, Quilter's Year
Block Party Series 2, Baskets & Flowers
Block Party Series 3, Quilters Almanac
Block Party Series 4, Christmas Traditions
Block Party Series 5, Pioneer Sampler
Block Party Series 6, Applique in a Day
Block Party Series 7, Stars Across America
Town Square Sampler

Angle Piecing

Diamond Log Cabin Tablecloth or Treeskirt
Pineapple Quilt
Blazing Star Tablecloth
Schoolhouse Quilt
Radiant Star Quilt

Quilt in a Day®, Inc. • 1955 Diamond Street • San Marcos, CA 92069
1 800 777-4852 • Fax: (760) 591-4424 • www.quiltinaday.com